BECOMING
REVOLUTIONARY

BECOMING REVOLUTIONARY

ANALISA TURNOW &
JILLIAN MARIE

© 2021 by Analisa Turnow and Jillian Marie. All rights reserved.

Published by Redemption Press, PO Box 427, Enumclaw, WA 98022.

Toll-Free (844) 2REDEEM (273-3336)

Redemption Press is honored to present this title in partnership with the author. The views expressed or implied in this work are those of the author. Redemption Press provides our imprint seal representing design excellence, creative content, and high quality production.

No part of this publication may be reproduced, stored in a retrieval system, or transmitted in any way by any means—electronic, mechanical, photocopy, recording, or otherwise—without the prior permission of the copyright holder, except as provided by USA copyright law.

The author has tried to recreate events, locales, and conversations from memories of them. In order to maintain their anonymity, in some instances the names of individuals are changed and some identifying characteristics and details may have changed, such as physical properties, occupations, and places of residence.

Non-commercial interests may reproduce portions of this book without the express written permission of authors, provided the text does not exceed 500 words. When reproducing text from this book, include the following credit line: "Becoming Revolutionary by Analisa Turnow and Jillian Marie. Used by permission."

Commercial interests: No part of this publication may be reproduced in any form, stored in a retrieval system, or transmitted in any form by any means—electronic, photocopy, recording, or otherwise—without prior written permission of the publisher/author, except as provided by the United States of America copyright law.

Unless otherwise indicated, all Scripture quotations are taken from the Holy Bible, New International Version®, NIV®. Copyright © 1973, 1978, 1984, 2011 by Biblica, Inc.™ Used by permission of Zondervan. All rights reserved worldwide. www.zondervan.com The "NIV" and "New International Version" are trademarks registered in the United States Patent and Trademark Office by Biblica, Inc.™

Scripture quotations marked ESV® are taken from The Holy Bible, English Standard Version®), copyright © 2001 by Crossway, a publishing ministry of Good News Publishers. Used by permission. All rights reserved.

Scripture quotations marked NLT are taken from the Holy Bible, New Living Translation, copyright ©1996, 2004, 2015 by Tyndale House Foundation. Used by permission of Tyndale House Publishers, Carol Stream, Illinois 60188. All rights reserved.

Scripture quotations marked NLV are taken from the New Life Version, copyright © 1969 and 2003. Used by permission of Barbour Publishing, Inc., Uhrichsville, Ohio 44683. All rights reserved.

ISBN 13: 978-1-64645-086-2 (Paperback)
978-1-64645-087-9 (ePub)
978-1-64645-088-6 (Mobi)

Library of Congress Catalog Card Number: 2020921502

Contents

Chapter 1: Becoming Eve	9
Chapter 2: Doubt	15
Chapter 3: False Fantasy and Sin	21
Chapter 4: The Consequence—Shame and Hiding	33
Chapter 5: Facing Our Dysfunction	41
Chapter 6: The Hope of Redemption	49
Chapter 7: Becoming Revolutionary	53

Preface

Revolution is meant to bring about change. This book is intended to reveal a personal revolution—a revolution that can happen in your heart, mind, and soul. This is not a book about becoming greater, better, stronger, more influential, or more powerful. Its rudimentary writings are meant to spark contemplation of the parts of your soul you may not like to examine. It will challenge your way of thinking so that you are not defined by your mistakes and deficiencies but, rather, so you can determine those things that bring hope, love, and identity to your very being. We believe that is a revolutionary response to a pandemic belief.

CHAPTER 1

Becoming Eve

Eve's story is not for the faint of heart. She makes us search our own hearts, minds, souls, and intentions. She makes us go back to the beginning, our beginning—the start of our deficiency, doubt, and shame. Her story is our story, even if we don't like to admit it. I would argue that Eve would probably be the best woman to seek advice from when confronted with sin. No other woman has ever experienced so fully both sides of humanity. She experienced perfection and then suffered through the pain of losing everything and dying in brokenness. She understood more than anyone how sinful and flawed we really are. She recognized how deep sin goes and how far it separates us from the perfection that God intended for us. She experienced how sin starts and the devastation it can bring.

Eve was created perfect. She lived in complete innocence. She lived, for a moment, without any shame. Genesis tells us she was naked and unashamed in Adam's presence as well as God's. She experienced what we all dream of and hope for—complete and utter freedom. Yet that was all she had ever known. We all face a moment, as Eve did, when we give into our own desires and forfeit our innocence and freedom for the false promises of something more.

We know Eve's story: she was deceived by the Serpent, she took the fruit, and she lost everything. Instantly her life changed forever, with eternal consequences for all who came after her—consequences we face and live with to this day. Gone is the perfection she was created in, and in its place is the lifelong battle of pain, shame, guilt, sin, inadequacy, hiding, and striving.

But I imagine she always remembered those moments in the garden with the ache of what once was burdening her soul and thoughts of the wonders she had once been privileged enough to live in. Eve started with everything and, therefore, experienced the greatest loss that anyone could ever have. She knew the ultimate consequence of sin because she immediately experienced the separation between her and God and the shame it brought. She had everything to lose and she did. Her striving for perfection led to the starvation of her soul.

It is in the response to her loss that revolutionary things began to happen. Rather than tossed out and disregarded, God gave Eve and Adam hope. The stage was set, and a loving Creator looked upon humanity with compassion, love, and mercy. We give Eve revolutionary status because the Bible tells us her legacy, and her response to loss, opposes what we would expect. In Eve's sin and brokenness, her hope was restored in God.

Like most revolutionary women, we start with nothing and must learn to defy the odds against us. During times of struggle, it is the revolutionary woman's faith in God and His promises for her life that enable her to persevere through pain. She remains faithful in periods of waiting, in times of struggle, and during the unknown because of eternal hope that was promised from the beginning.

Eve's life is in reverse. Living in the shadow of perfection of what once was, she learned how to keep going—a lesson all generations thereafter will follow. She battled sin, shame, and guilt, and it is through her story we can ask ourselves the same thing she must have asked herself: How do I understand the depths of my sin and experience shame and guilt, yet live a life filled with hope, purpose, redemption, and freedom? This question, if allowed to stir within us, can be the beginning of a revolutionary work where we do not have to be defined by our mistakes but can have a new identity that never wavers, withstands any trial, and gives us eternal hope and purpose.

It took me a very long time to connect with Eve and her story because I did not want to look in the mirror and see myself as Eve. I saw myself as a consequence of Eve's sin, having to live in sin as my fate. Of course, I knew I sinned, but I did not like to imagine myself as flawed as Eve and have to carry the weight of being the one who forfeited living in perfection. I've repeatedly told myself I would never go back to the relationship that left me feeling used. I've told myself, "I would never sacrifice all of that for a piece of fruit." Yet if I really look at my life and decisions, I see that I do it all the time. I forfeit the promise that God has offered simply to fulfill a temporary desire that will only leave me wishing I had never done it in the first place. This realization has allowed me to begin relating to Eve. I know I am sinful and flawed, but there is always the option to curse and blame Eve for that infamous moment that changed the course of humanity and is responsible for my brokenness and sinful ways.

> And he said, "Who told you that you were naked? Have you eaten from the tree that I commanded you not to eat from?" The man said, "The woman you put here with me—she gave me some fruit from the tree, and I ate it." Then the Lord God said to the woman, "What is this you have done?" The woman said, "The serpent deceived me, and I ate." (Genesis 3:11–13)

How ironic that I would scrutinize Adam and Eve, yet my first response to my sin is identical to that of Adam and Eve—to make excuses rather than see the destruction of my own decisions, actions, and thought patterns. Adam and Eve tried to shift the blame onto someone else. Adam blamed Eve, Eve blamed the Serpent, and I blame them. And finally the time comes when we separate ourselves from the blaming and begin unveiling the root of our actions, disobedience, selfishness, and ultimately sin. Relating to Eve becomes less and less difficult.

Identifying with Eve, allowing ourselves to enter her story and see our similarities, may be a catalyst to understanding the source of our own struggles. By allowing her story to penetrate into the deepest parts of our souls, we can begin to understand the depths of her battle and flaws so that we can start to identify our own, for the root is the same. Eve's struggle with doubt and desire to satisfy selfish cravings produced neither clarity nor power but a life clouded in labor and torment. We, too, live in the same world of doubt and unrelenting pursuit of achievement, success, power, financial security, love, and acceptance that never fully fulfills but leaves us yearning for more.

To study her life exposes our vulnerabilities. It exposes our own shame and regret. It makes us see that we truly are no different. And if we are no different, then we are not alone in this struggle. The process is hard. But if we are willing to be honest with ourselves—owning our pain, shame, guilt, hiding, and fear—we can begin unveiling our true story in hopes of living in freedom, rather than a buried, detached, and isolated livelihood. If we fail to understand the depth of our sin and need for a Savior, we will fail to experience the profoundness of His provision. To pass up the opportunity to fight means to miss the power, beauty, and hope that comes completely undeserved, yet is only received when we understand that we really need it.

The question becomes, "Do I want to understand my sin and the root of my sin?" It is by understanding and exposing the roots of sin that strongholds can be broken. We can be free from blaming and pivoting from one dysfunctional situation to the next. We can live a life of experiencing God's grace and mercy and walk alongside him, feeling no shame once again. This intimacy is offered to us freely, and we must soften our hearts in humility to receive it.

This battle is not what it seems. It is an unconventional fight because there is a predeclared victory and known victor who fought on our behalf to free us from our pain, shame, guilt, hiding, and fear.

> He was despised and rejected by mankind, a man of suffering, and familiar with pain. Like one from whom people hide their faces, he was despised, and we held him in low esteem. Surely he took up our pain and bore our suffering, yet we considered him punished by God, stricken by him, and afflicted. But he was pierced for our transgressions, he was crushed for our iniquities; the punishment that brought us peace was on him, and by his wounds we are healed. (Isaiah 53:3–5)

CHAPTER 2

Doubt

Now the serpent was more crafty than any other beast of the field that the Lord God had made. He said to the woman, "Did God actually say, 'You shall not eat of any tree in the garden'?" And the woman said to the serpent, "We may eat of the fruit of the trees in the garden, but God said, 'You shall not eat of the tree that is in the midst of the garden, neither shall you touch it, lest you die.'"
Genesis 3:1–3

Just as this story is centered in the garden, so this battle is central to our lives. How we engage God and face sin and temptation is essential to who we are, how we will live life on this earth, and who we will become. We see in this passage from Genesis 3 that though we are to have God at the center, Satan does not retreat from this place but, instead, attacks at the core. The conversation with the Serpent changed Adam and Eve's certainty to doubt that penetrated through their defenses into the most sacred and central part of themselves. Adam and Eve, once confident in who God was, allowed doubt to skew their perspective of God's plan and love for them. Starting off with good intentions and pure motives, they allowed the Serpent to break their defenses and cause them to doubt the perfection, purpose, and communion they had with God.

Eve had been confident in the perfection of her circumstances, but her resolve was challenged. It began with the question, "Did

God actually say . . . ?" Disbelief, distrust, confusion, fear, and ultimately selfishness seeped in and clouded what had seemed so sure and true.

Our questions have the same effect on our faith, certainty, and conviction. Does God really love me? Is he really the God of freedom? Does he really have the best for me? Can I succeed without God? Can I be in control of my own destiny? It is an anti-God mentality. With Eve's choice to eat the fruit, she chose to become her own god. For us, too, it's the belief that we don't have enough. It's wanting to control the unknown. The Serpent knew how to attack Eve with doubt. He is described as the most cunning and clever beast created. We are told in 1 Peter 5:8–9 that the devil, our enemy, prowls around looking for someone to devour and kill.

Satan manipulates and takes God's truth and twists it for self-righteousness. Just like a snake, Satan uses invisibility and silence to camouflage himself. As he approached Eve, he appeared innocent and nonthreatening. Be aware that he is relentless with his motives and tactics, stopping at nothing to complete his mission of devouring us and separating us from God's love and mercy. He waits for his prey to be vulnerable. For Eve, she was alone, and for Adam, Satan used the person who was closest to him to challenge him and soften his defenses. Satan approaches without warning, appearing harmless at first. But he strikes with deadly precision, using the venom of pride and doubt. He attacks from the outside and lets the questions do their work on the inside of us. These inner struggles set up a home, seeping in and allowing the poison to spread to the places of vulnerability within and then destroying us. When we give into his attack and engage the lies, we allow them to become deadly.

When Satan questioned Eve about God's instructions not to eat from the tree, she responded, "We may eat of the fruit of the trees in the garden, but God said, 'You shall not eat of the fruit of the tree that is in the midst of the garden, neither shall you touch it, lest you die'" (Genesis 3:2–3 ESV). God's command in Genesis

2:16–17 (ESV) says, "You may surely eat of every tree of the garden, but of the tree of the knowledge of good and evil you shall not eat, for in the day that you eat of it you will surely die."

Eve allowed the doubt the Serpent posed to enter her mind. Satan presented the question by taking what God had made positive and making it negative. (He had offered everything in the garden except that which would harm them.) Eve was the one who distorted the command within her mind. At first she combatted it with truth, but then she added to it, which changes everything. She set herself up to allow even more doubt to come in, which Satan always capitalizes on. "But the serpent said to the woman, 'You will not surely die. For God knows that when you eat of it your eyes will be opened and you will be like God, knowing good and evil." (Genesis 3:4–5 ESV).

Eve engaged the Serpent. She focused on God's one restriction in her life and became blinded to the limitless freedom intended for her. The devil mixed truth with deceit, and Eve believed the lie that she would be raised to godlike status, revealing an idol in every human heart—the idol of self-elevation. *Satan mixes truth with fallacy to create a fantasy.* And instead of being raised up to be like her Creator, as Eve thinks will happen with eating the fruit, it makes her like Satan.

When Eve ate, her innocence was forfeited, and her eyes were opened to sin, pain, and shame . . . things God never intended humans to experience. Doubt and pride can blind us to reality, just as it did to Eve. Reason and conviction battle emotion and imagination when we are tempted. Our pulse begins to quicken, and our senses take over, silencing all reasoning. Doubt creeps in—doubt in God, doubt in the future, doubt in the effects of sin, and ultimately doubt of identity. We hope for something better than what can be seen or experienced. We reach for something tangible. We desire something to validate our purpose, acceptance, and superiority.

Doubt never stops attacking us. It will always be a part of our lives. Stop and think about how many times in the last hour you have doubted who you are, what your purpose is, what you think you should have, or where you should be in life. Now compound that in a day, a week, a month, a year, a lifetime. Doubt is important to identify because it is the very thing that makes you question your identity. And when you question your identity, it opens the door to redefine yourself by what you are lacking or what you have compared to others.

Doubt left unchecked and unchallenged will always elicit the same response as Eve's. We reach out and take the fruit before us, becoming the product of our own ambition and left in the consequences of sin. And that leaves us longing for the innocence lost by giving into sin.

Doubt also questions truth and our purpose. It falsely mitigates the consequences of our actions by creating an illusion of what will be gained. With doubt, there is a choice: challenge it or give into it. Eve gave into the doubt, reached out, took the fruit, and ate it. How we reach out may be different for each of us. What we strive for and give into is particular to our own experiences, desires, and longings. Our sin takes on three different categories: the lust of the flesh, the lust of the eyes, and inner pride. Reaching out may look like pursuing destructive relationships, participating in indulgent behaviors, isolating ourselves, or overworking to control, avoid, or escape. This list could go on, but regardless of the vice, if we consume it and believe that it will give us satisfaction and fulfillment, we will be left longing for something more.

In the midst of doubt, we search for answers and are faced with constant choices. The patterns of our choices may reveal how we try to combat our doubt and the motives of our desires. We can fight with our own desires, or we can switch perspectives and fight in line with how God empowers us to live when we trust him. When we begin to live by faith, we start to trust that what God has for us is greater than the shadow of doubt that feeds into our own self-glorifying and self-gratifying nature. James 1:6 says that when we doubt we are like a wave of the sea, blown and tossed by the wind. When anything challenges our conviction or identity as who God says we are, we can either be steadfast and grounded in truth, or we can give into doubt and be tossed back and forth between faith and uncertainty—a struggle that we think gives us control but actually leaves us treading water.

The purpose of understanding doubt is to discern how we forfeit the good things God has in our lives. By recognizing how doubt does its work inside us, we can then learn to combat it. It is a spiritual battle. As much as Satan is the predator waiting to strike us, which he does, we can have the firmness of mind to identify the lies. But, to do so, we must have a foundation of truth and trust in who God really is. Without it, we will inevitably fail.

Acknowledge and be aware that Satan wants to destroy you. He will attack and he is clever. But through Jesus Christ you can live in freedom and have confidence that withstands any question or doubt. To know Jesus is to understand love. The disciple John says, "But anyone who does not love does not know God, for God is love" (1 John 4:8 NLT) and, "We know how much God loves us, and we have put our trust in his love. God is love, and all who live in love live in God, and God lives in them" (1 John 4:16 NLT).

Doubt is a consistent emotion the human race has faced from the beginning of time. For Eve, this doubt caused her to forfeit her perfection. She lost her perfect life in the perfect garden with a perfect God. This cycle of doubt began with a question, "Did God really say . . . ?" This question hit Eve at the core, leaving her with an image of what she thought perfection could be instead of what perfection already was. Eve's mentality of always striving for more led her into a dangerous conversation with Satan, and she was deceived in the same way he tries to deceive us: *he mixes truth with fallacy to create a fantasy.*

~ CHAPTER 3 ~

False Fantasy and Sin

"You will certainly not die," the serpent said to the woman. For God knows that when you eat from it your eyes will be opened, and you will be like God, knowing good and evil. When the woman saw that the fruit of the tree was good for food and pleasing to the eye, and also desirable for gaining wisdom, she took some and ate it. She also gave some to her husband, who was with her, and he ate it.
Genesis 3:4–6

Doubt by itself is not enough to forfeit the promises of God and to cause us to make choices that are self-glorifying and self-gratifying and ultimately result in sin. Doubt can lead us toward sin if we allow questions, fear, and the unknown to drive our minds and actions. When we give into doubt, we can quickly allow our minds to give into false fantasies and fears that lead us to question the goodness of God. When I doubt the promises of God, I believe there is something better for me. When I doubt my value and identity, I put my worth into something that I anticipate will bring greater fulfillment.

Galatians 5:17 says, "For the flesh desires what is contrary to the Spirit, and the Spirit what is contrary to the flesh. They are in conflict with each other, so that you are not to do whatever you want." Satan capitalizes on this inner conflict by continually challenging the desires of our flesh (pride, sexual intimacy, drunkenness, power, success at any cost, selfishness, etc.) and by making our own desires seem so much better and fulfilling than the alternative. The playback could look like the following:

1. You search for intimacy with someone or multiple people to make you feel desired and loved. Common mindsets and snares may include: "At least I have someone." "No one else will love me." "At least I can feel something. I have felt numb for so long." Whether it's staying in an unhealthy relationship, sitting in fear and misery, or holding onto bitterness and resentment, beware of keeping yourself in chains rather than stepping out into the unknown and trusting that God can do his healing work.

2. You believe the lies: "I am not good enough, smart enough, strong enough, pretty enough, etc." You give yourself over to striving at any cost, leading to an excessive focus on self. You begin to compare yourself to anyone and everyone, leading to an inner resentment of others and of yourself. The world's standards leave you empty because there is always someone who will be "superior" to you.

3. You become blinded to your own self-entitlement mentality with a prideful stance that excuses you from fault from your actions, opinions, and excuses. You take on the mindset that your circumstances, identity, success, and brokenness are not in your control. This mindset tells you there is no hope and there is nothing you can do to break free from your pain or shame. You are left in chains—the chains of fear, misery, bitterness, and resentment. Your inner being begins to beg the question: "How could they leave me?" "They will never find anyone better." "I deserve the success after all I have been through."

In Genesis, Satan attacks Eve by planting the seed of desire and fantasy. He uses this tactic not just with Eve but also when he tempts Jesus in Matthew 4. Satan reuses old schemes over and over to bait us outside the will of God. Satan *mixes truth with fallacy to create a false sense of fantasy* that leads to self-glorification and self-gratification. He brings to the surface this inner battle.

Fantasy occurs in the mind and reveals the desires of our hearts. It consumes our thoughts and actions. It steals our energy and our time. It can change our purpose and cause us to compromise. Fantasy makes us reprioritize what we think is important. What we fantasize about becomes an idol, and it will seep out into our actions and motives. The Bible cautions us to guard our hearts. Proverbs 4:23 says, "Above all guard your heart, for everything you do flows from it."

Your mind, your thought processes, your words, and your actions are all influenced by your heart. Where is your heart centered? Do you want the primary desire of your life to be for the creation or the Creator? Is what I am dreaming about a true promise of God, or is it something that only brings self-glorification or gratification?

What happens to your mental state when you are consumed with fantasies?

1. It opens you up to bitterness. Bitterness leads to resentment, resentment to anger, anger to compromise, and compromise back to bitterness.
2. It makes you angry at God for not getting the desire of your heart.
3. It steals your time and energy.
4. It keeps you from desiring things that should be a priority.
5. It often leads to compromise.
6. It may cause you to miss an opportunity in front of you.
7. It keeps you from pouring into others and making new, meaningful relationships.
8. It isolates you and leaves you susceptible to Satan.
9. It leads to deeper sin.

Knowing your doubts, areas of weakness, vulnerabilities, and how you let yourself fantasize can help reveal your motives and identify the root of the desire. But combating these things can seem impossible at times. Developing true change is difficult. No self-help book, no amount of self-improvement, no amount of religious rhetoric will get you to the place of self-sustaining enlightenment.

It is impossible to live a life that is pure and faultless on your own, constantly combating doubt, fantasy, and identity. Is it a battle worth fighting?

An excerpt from a friend writing about this very topic reveals the inner battle many of us deal with when confronted with fantasy and sin:

> Within the sin patterns I heard a voice, seemingly subconscious, telling me the subtle lies. Enticing me with the false sense of fantasy to ignite curiosity. Within this moment the opportunity for escape reveals itself. The Spirit sends warnings yet the deeper I entangle myself with hidden idols, the more I become numb to my emotion. It is in this I have become my own god. I become a master at silencing caution and living within the resentment of God, of others, and of myself. I have lived in places of fantasy far too often and come out void every time. The Serpent is deceptive indeed and is no respecter of persons. He will use those closest to you to create dysfunction to come out within. The best scheme of Satan is to use my own thoughts, feelings, and intellectual ability to destroy myself from the inside out. Satan does not need to do much, just one half-truth from a sin pattern ten years ago is enough to cause a world of self-inflicted dysfunction. But this is what I have discovered: the response to shame, guilt, and remorse is praise. The deeper the shame, the more passionate the praise. My sanity hinges on Christ's sanctity. (Used with permission.)

Why do we struggle with fantasy? When our minds go into fantasy, the thought process varies rapidly from moment to moment. I can be on the treadmill dreaming about what I am believing God for in my life. But before my thirty-minute workout is complete, I have played out the next ten years of my life, complete with the dream house, the perfect family, and a boatload of cash in the bank! Fantasy takes us to a subconscious state of imagination.

Our thought process can also take this same shape when we think about our faith and what we believe God will do in our lives. For me, I begin to fantasize about what I want God to do in my life and, instead of glorifying the perfect Savior no matter the circumstances, I end up manipulating God; I subtly become my own god again. This state of mind begins to drive my thought process, and I find myself wanting to stay longer and longer in my fantasy mindset to escape the reality of what I do not have or the reality of being on that treadmill! I dare say this state of mind is as dangerous as escaping from reality with alcohol, avoidance of tasks, or alienation of self.

How do we know when we are using avoidance tactics to guard ourselves or escape the reality of a less than stellar day? Fantasy is far from reality and will lead to reaching and reacting to people and situations God never intended. When we fall short of our fantasy that was so beautifully played out in our heads or face an unexpected rejection or place expectations on others they were never meant to carry, we blame God. The truth is, God refuses to step into our false fantasies, because he already stepped into our struggles by sending his son Jesus. And instead of giving into false fantasy offered to him by Satan, he willingly gave up his life so that we could have eternity with him and the brokenness of the garden could be restored. The questions now shift to: Does your desire become total reliance on God and the total surrender of self? Is he worth your complete desire?

We dream. We hope. We imagine. These are not bad things. In fact, we are created with these abilities. That is what makes us unique from the rest of God's creation. If we settled for where we are, we would never become who we were created to be—like Eve, naked in the garden walking with the Creator. The problem is our hidden desire to become our own god rather than desiring God above all else.

God can take you from your sinful self and make you new. Know that he can also do that with your thoughts. He can give you new hope and new desire by guarding your heart and filling it with things that give you new focus. He can fill your heart with things that bring life and joy and true obedience in Christ, instead of the things of the world.

Our fantasies can put us in holding patterns and make us anxious about life. False fantasies are not just the positive things we hope for. False fantasies can be those thoughts that make us anxious or afraid. We do both. We give into the scenarios that we think will make us happy and complete, such as fantasies of having money, being successful, becoming a parent, getting a promotion, or anything that is completely self-fulfilling for our own identity and affirmation. Or our fantasies can be negative—things we envision will devastate us if they happen—worrying if we do *this*, people will think *that*, or if *this* happens, I will lose *that*.

Proactively guard your heart but know that you are not alone! "Do not be anxious about anything, but in every situation, by prayer and petition, with thanksgiving, present your request to God. And the peace of God, which transcends all understanding, will guard your hearts and your minds in Christ Jesus" (Philippians 4:6–7).

When we ask God to help us change our false fantasies and fix our minds on what is true, he steps into our lives. He comes alongside us and helps protect our minds from ourselves. He lets us exchange false fantasies for truth, which means fixing our minds on how we can glorify God in every aspect of our lives. We must start the work for true change, and it begins with our minds. "Finally, brothers and sisters, whatever is true, whatever is noble, whatever is right, whatever is pure, whatever is lovely, whatever is admirable—if anything is excellent or praiseworthy—think about such things" (Philippians 4:8).

The beauty of guarding our hearts is that each person will learn how to do this for themselves in different ways. Personal struggles and questions are unique to each of us. Learning how to combat doubt and guard our hearts will be unique as well. That is what gives us diverse abilities and purposes.

Guarding your heart is a spiritual discipline. It takes practice and a proactive mind. But ultimately it takes humility in coming

FALSE FANTASY AND SIN

before the Lord and allowing him to reveal your sin and the idols of your false fantasies.

We will always default to fulfilling our fantasy and letting our own desires lead our thoughts and actions. For change to occur, it requires the work of the Holy Spirit inside of us to reveal these areas we hold onto. With the power that God gives us, we can shift perspective so that our sole desire is to keep our minds renewed in the ways of God and move our thoughts away from self to thoughts on Christ. It takes time. To be proficient in anything requires time and attention.

How, then, do we soften our hearts to allow the Holy Spirit to come in and meet us where we are? Following are examples of practical ways God gives us in Scripture to be able to meet with him, seek him and his truth, and live life with other believers. These are not steps to accomplish that allow us to work our way to him but, rather, steps to check if we are allowing him to be in every part of our lives.

1. Read Scripture. Knowing his Word is vital to knowing God personally and knowing his character. Read Scripture through the lens that the Bible is the story of the gospel in every way and is meant to glorify God, save you, and show you how to live through struggles on earth with eternal purpose.

    a. It resets focus on your Creator and not on what you can create or manufacture.
    b. It brings you back to the truth, because when your fantasies mix with your thought patterns, you cannot discern the difference.
    c. It reminds you of the character of God: that he is loving, merciful, good, gracious, a pursuer of your soul, and wants the best for you even if it means saying *no*.
    d. It shows you time and again that he is consistent.

e. It establishes the standard of love and reveals how everything else falls short.

2. Take the time to self-evaluate and check your motives and actions. This is not a book on time management; it is about discovering the love relationship with a Savior who wants you to experience freedom and true love to the point that it overflows into every aspect of your life. In your relationships. In your time. In your thoughts. In your dreams.

    Understanding the purpose of your life is vital to knowing how to endure the inevitable struggles of doubt and comparison perpetuated by human nature and a society that beckons us to fantasize about things that ultimately will not matter. Your purpose hinges solely on your identity with Christ. Anything that pulls on that identity is fantasy.

    So is your life in a holding pattern that seems like your schedule is out of control and you are left falling short of who you are created to be? It does not mean that you change jobs. It does not mean that you change your marital status. You can experience deeper intimacy with Christ that transforms how you live each busy day. Your time in and of itself can reveal your desires. Is your day oriented to be filled as a distraction from your inner self, or do you focus on others and allow space for God to meet you every day? What would happen if your priorities changed in a way that allowed you to discover who God is and who you are? What would happen if you gave yourself the time to rediscover your potential and step into it in a new way? What would happen if when you are fatigued, you press into something real that will sustain you, instead of striving or shutting down in front of a screen?

Only you can discover what this looks like in your life. But to truly exist and live a revolutionary life takes effort. It can feel cumbersome, but he will meet you as soon as you call upon him to do so. All he wants is to give you that, and he is waiting to meet you exactly where you are. But he wants all of you. And he is there waiting for the instant you desire him more than all those other things calling your name (Proverbs 31).

3. Surround yourself with people who love God and speak truth. This can be manifested in different ways, often in friendships or mentorship. Though you need many types of relationships in your life, it is critical to have people to encourage you and speak truth into your life. Find those people who can love you when you cannot love yourself, those who speak truth even when it is hard to say, those who encourage you, and those who pray with you. These are rare relationships of just one or two people, and not mere casual friendships.

    Guard your heart and be extremely protective about who speaks into your life so that you can discern when others are feeding into your struggles and false fantasies. There are probably many people in your life who only cast further doubt and pull you into comparison and false fantasies. It is very difficult to combat lies without the influence of friends who speak truth.

4. Ask God to reveal your sin and bring your struggles to the surface so that you can be deeply changed in Christ. Exchanging false fantasies and shortcomings with self-help strategies, lists of religious steps (just pray more and read the Bible more), and resolutions to be a better person will ultimately lead to the exact same complex. Each of these lead to striving and falling short and perpetuate a cycle of anxiety, leading back to

the original complex that we see with Eve. The cycle will leave you desiring to stay in control, desiring false fantasies, and desiring things that bring self-fulfillment and self-gratification.

But in Scripture, we see how Jesus came down to break this cycle so that we could all be restored to original wholeness and purpose. He was perfect when we could not be. When tempted, instead of giving in to false fantasy, he remained righteous and used truth to combat all the things we face. He did not step into sinful patterns but overcame every struggle so that we could rely on him in our struggles. While perfect he died so we would become perfect too. Through his sacrifice, he allows us to step outside the cycle, and he gives us everything we need to endure the millions of doubts thrown at us every day. The victory he has over sin is extended to us freely.

Is he worth letting go of your false fantasies and your own patterns of comfort and control? His love is the true sacrificial love that allows you and me to step out of the cycle, not by any works of our own, but by his power, perfection, love, and mercy.

For those who have been waiting for a fantasy and believing it is faith, remember that faith is not the belief that what you want will come true. Faith is the trust in God who is above our thoughts, our motives, and our intentions. Life is filled with "gaps" between the anticipation of what life would be like and how it has played out. The gap always requires God's grace to permeate through our souls to begin healing the pain of unmet expectations. When we experience unmet expectations, we can reach for things that try to fulfill us or we can allow God to change our desires and be fully fulfilled in him alone.

FALSE FANTASY AND SIN

Eve reaching for the fruit left us in a world of consequence that leaves us constantly reaching for those things that won't fulfill us. The cycle of doubt and false fantasy often leads to that act of sin and dysfunction. We can find ourselves in a perpetual cycle of dysfunction: doubt, false fantasy, reaching, and sinning to result in our own shame and hiding. Eve was the first to experience this perpetual cycle: the up and down of perfection and grace to destruction and self-hate. The fruit was easy to take and we have the freedom to take it, yet the consequences last a lifetime.

CHAPTER 4

The Consequence—Shame and Hiding

Then the eyes of both of them were opened, and they realized they were naked; so they sewed fig leaves together and made coverings for themselves. Then the man and his wife heard the sound of the Lord God as he was walking in the garden in the cool of the day, and they hid from the Lord God among the trees of the garden. But the Lord God called to the man, "Where are you?" The man answered, "I heard you in the garden, and I was afraid because I was naked; so I hid." And God said, "Who told you that you were naked? Have you eaten from the tree that I commanded you not to eat from?" The man said, "The woman you put here with me—she gave me some fruit from the tree, and I ate it." Then the Lord God said to the woman, "What is this you have done?" The woman said, "The serpent deceived me, and I ate."
Genesis 3:7–13 NIV

For Eve and Adam, the pathway of sin began with doubt and ended in shame and hiding. Doubt questions truth and our purpose, mitigates the consequences of our actions, and creates a false sense of what will be gained. When faced with a change in circumstance or emotion, doubt challenges our convictions, making it easier to concede who we are and give ourselves over to sin. Sin immediately opens our eyes to our own disgrace and regret, leading to shame. In our shame we hide and try to cover ourselves because we are now vulnerable. Inevitably we are left living in the reality that what we were meant for is not who we are now.

Genesis 3:7 says, "Then the eyes of both of them were opened, and they realized they were naked; so they sewed fig leaves together and made coverings for themselves." The first experience after eating the fruit was shame. The feeling of innocence and safety was gone. They are not ashamed because of any imperfection in their bodies, for that did not change. They are ashamed because now when they look at each other, perfect trust and love have been shattered. The purity has been stripped from the lives of both Adam and Eve as they realize the vulnerability and perfection that was weaved into the essence of who they are has now been skewed.

Shame does not come from our nakedness or exposure; shame comes from sin. The only thing that shifted was perspective. God remained the same. Adam and Eve's shame in sin was self-inflicted and self-imposed and made them self-absorbed. The chasm between how they were created and what they now were made them feel ashamed. They covered themselves, showing that perfect trust between them was broken and experiencing a new fear of how they believed God would respond.

As Eve realized her sin and disobedience, hiding seemed like the protective thing to do. Eve knew how far she had fallen from the dreams God had spoken over her, and in sin and shame her feelings of self-loathing further separated her from God. Hiding isolates us from those around us who love us and separates us from God's saving and healing grace. Isolation often ends up making us feel more alone and vulnerable rather than giving us the protection we desire. In isolation, the hiding becomes easier and the thoughts of shame can run rampant.

Sin beckons us to forego our innocence and, ultimately, will leave us wounded and in a state of covering. Shame and hiding become a revolving door. The trap of hiding is appealing because it falsely provides a fleeting feeling of protection and healing. The

THE CONSEQUENCE—SHAME AND HIDING

defense mechanism in hiding tells us to shove down shame to the deepest places in our heart and bury it so we can try to control everything else and attempt to move forward. But, in fact, the opposite is true.

Shame and hiding feed on each other and keep us separated, leading to greater and deeper bondage, and further burying and isolating. We think our sin and shame will go away if we bury them. Burying our sin and shame can also leave us feeling in control for the time being, until we have to deal with the ramifications later. Burying sin and shame is a false solution because it keeps us from one of the most important things we can do for ourselves: being honest. Undealt with shame and hiding can become our identity. We think if we bury it, it will die off. But really it kills our soul. It kills our spirit. It kills our purpose.

In hiding, we set ourselves up for living in separation and isolation. Hiding can be a passive process of withdrawing from others, ourselves, and God. Hiding can be a reflex to sin and shame, unconsciously pulling into ourselves and building a wall. Or hiding can be active, deliberately running from situations and avoiding consequences of our actions. We feel as though we are taking action by hiding. We think we can run from the situation we created and, even more, become invisible to God. Yet the Lord will call us by name in this season every time. For example, a child who disobeys runs and hides in fear and shame. The child's response is to hide and stay silent, yet the parent will lovingly go to bring the child out of a place of hiding. A parent's love does not want that sin to remain covered and the child to live in hiding and fear. Exposing the sin can ultimately free the child to experience the parent's forgiveness and love. Forgiveness does not mean absence of consequences, but it allows for the cost of sin to be covered and the child to be free from shame, no longer needing to hide.

The purpose of identifying sin, shame, and hiding is to see that a natural response has been paid and covered. There is always a cost to sin. That cost can be separation, isolation, hiding, and ultimately death. Or if you believe Jesus paid that penalty to pull the sinner out of hiding and free from shame, that becomes the choice.

When we begin to hide in the midst of our sin, others can see our dysfunction. Adam and Eve heard God coming and *then* they hid. They were standing in the open, exposed to the sin and could not even see their shame until they heard the God of the universe coming close. That is why Adam and Eve hid, and this is why we continue to hide. We hide because God's proximity in our lives exposes sin as the death trap it truly is. We hide from God because it is easier than facing him. When we face God with our inadequacies, he begins to equip us to expose it for ourselves, identifying the root cause that was never from God to begin with. When we allow God to draw near, he does not demand anything, but he compels our hearts to change through his perfect love.

Everything that is hidden within our lives will be revealed. The covering is the beginning of pretending. Just as Eve was exposed, our sin will also be exposed and unveil the idols held within our hearts. We do not spend a lot of time hiding in trees as Eve did, so what does hiding look like today?

Attempts to physically cover sin could manifest in the following ways:

- Drastic changes to appearance, such as grooming, using clothes to cover the entire body, extreme differences in hair color and haircut, etc.
- Weight fluctuations
- Missed work
- Excess sleeping
- Fits of rage
- Promiscuity
- Extreme exercising

Attempts to emotionally cover sin could result in:

THE CONSEQUENCE—SHAME AND HIDING

- Chronic crying
- Indifference and emotionlessness
- Fits of rage
- Manipulation of loved ones
- Prolonged absence
- Failure to keep promises
- Resentment toward others
- Hatred of self

Attempts to spiritually cover sin could look like:

- Resistance to godly advice for change
- Anger toward anyone wanting to set up parameters for your life
- Ceasing to tithe
- Distance from God
- Resentment toward God

So the question remains: How do you allow God to begin to change your natural patterns? You must recognize the dysfunction, process it, and allow it to cleanse and heal, or it will come out in all sorts of perverse ways. Identify what you run to in your state of hiding. Hiding places can be within your heart—the places that you do not physically run to as Eve did—but the places you emotionally hide behind to cover your true self.

We blame others for everything that goes wrong in our lives to sidestep the responsibility of facing our current realities. Emotional hiding places can be indicated by dissecting patterns of dysfunction within our lives. We circle around the dysfunction, never broaching the shame that is the foundation of our hiding. Designate in advance potential hiding places to break the cycle.

We can stay hidden in the darkness of our sin or step out into the light of grace and forgiveness that is freely offered to us. And when Eve stepped out, she became revolutionary. She was not destroyed. And when we step out before the Lord, exposing our shame and weakness, we are covered and we are claimed as his. We are no longer alone, hiding, in despair. We are exposed through naked trust. We are delivered.

What is the reality of shame and hiding? The way you escape could lead to greater captivity. Where you go when you run is of the utmost importance. Sometimes what you run to will end up running you. Often the strongholds in my life are things that I willingly ran to for protection but resulted in feelings of rejection. What I thought would help me led me into greater despair. This appears to be a continuous cycle within my life. Shame leads to fear, fear to regret, regret to obscurity, obscurity to a focus on self, focus on self to scarcity, scarcity to shame, and the cycle repeats.

We all experience shame or will at some point in our lives. It is the first response to sin. And we all have sinned and will sin. Shame is important to experience, for it allows us to see that we are flawed and that we can never be perfect. Shame proclaims the need for a Savior. But when shame consumes us and leads us to guilt and hiding, we strip the purpose of understanding our sin. Understanding our sin will either lead us to the feet of a Savior who already conquered it, or it will lead us to hide. And the false comfort and security found in hiding mocks us and keeps us in chains.

It is a lie that if we are hidden no one has to know. Hiding provides a false sense of strength, leading us to believe we can overcome on our own. Our default mechanisms of trying to hide our sin or cover it ourselves fall short because we are still left in the depravity of our sin. We have not fixed it, and we cannot fix it on our own. But we have the choice.

We see Eve move on and step out. We see her proclaiming the Lord in the birth of her children in Genesis 4:1. Eve could have stayed hidden. She could have stopped where she was. But she held onto the hope in Genesis 3 that her offspring would conquer the Serpent. She held onto knowing that the God who provided for her before was still present. And generations after her proclaim

God as the one true God. Perhaps we, too, have that choice. Does God give us mercy after we sin? Does God see past our hiding to the flawless person he created in the beginning?

Jesus is the sole place we can take refuge. With the Lord we can hide in plain sight because Jesus promises to be our shield and our protector. Freedom must always be fought for. If we want to be free from the sin patterns within our lives, staying close to Jesus is the first step and, I dare say, the hardest step to begin pinpointing the root of the sin. There is always a "why" for our behavior patterns and a reason we act as we do. The only way to self-diagnose is to dig. We must allow God to change us, and we must dig deep to get to the root of our dysfunction. Easier said than done, but healing physically, emotionally, and spiritually hinges on this crucial step.

CHAPTER 5

Facing Our Dysfunction

The thing about dysfunction is that it is hard to detect. Dysfunction wears so many different masks.

Eve engaged in conversation with the Serpent and began focusing on the one restriction in her life. Satan always attacks God's truth, and it caused Eve to question and doubt. She was blinded to the limitless freedom that had been set before her, not recognizing that the one restriction from God was for her ultimate protection.

The perception of Eve is intriguing. She lived in paradise. She walked with God in the garden and had every need met. She knew God was the Sustainer of all things. She knew that God was indeed the Creator of all things. And yet she found herself outside of the will of God, sewing fig leaves together to cover her outside being when, in actuality, it was her inner being that needed covering.

When we feel vulnerable or exposed in life, the immediate reaction is to hide from our issues, hide from the people we hurt, hide from God, and hide from ourselves. We compensate for falling short by trying to cover who we are and what we have done out of fear of judgment, punishment, and condemnation. In the end, we know this is what we really deserve.

The beauty of Genesis 3 is that the God Eve is running from is the same God who created the covering for Eve. God created the leaves that Eve used for her covering out of love and compassion for the hurt and guilt she was experiencing. God loves us so much he will do anything to cover our mistakes, so we can live in emotional, spiritual, and physical freedom.

Eve was born in perfection; we are born into sin. Eve had paradise and chose to propel herself to godlike status. We are born into Eve's sin and shame with the promise of perfection to come. To criticize Eve is detrimental to a woman's soul. Eve is a mirror to reflect self, not a story to be mocked. We are descendants of a great woman.

So why do we hide? We hide because it is easier than dealing with the root cause of the issue. It is far easier to bury the issue deep down and attempt to distinguish the feelings altogether. The funny thing about feelings is that they can rarely be trusted. Feelings alone lead us to quick reactions without thoughts of consequence. So we look at the ways we fall short and hate ourselves because of them. We look to change ourselves in any way we can and begin to once again reach for the forbidden fruit. We reach for anything that will quiet the dysfunction raging within our souls.

We have a choice within the moment of self-realization: to face it or to hide from it. We see Eve do both. First she hid from it because the initial reaction to being outside the will of God is to hide for fear of punishment. We know we deserve the punishment, but we are so selfish that when the thought of punishment comes, we try to cover ourselves with what is around us—significant others, jobs, kids, clothes, etc. Alcohol and drugs are a common escape because they allow us to temporarily separate from reality as well as from God. When the high wears off, the issues remain because the problems are still within us. The problems lie within our hearts, minds, and motives. Hiding is the easy way to temporarily escape from our problems, but it is in vain. When we hide we create more problems to compensate for the ones that have risen to the surface.

To face your issues means work. It is nose to the grindstone. It requires self-reflection and time with God. Most of all, facing your issues means facing yourself. It is being real with your Creator on the motives of your heart. Facing your dysfunction can be painful and bring consequences; we see this with Eve and the pain in bearing children. Yet, I dare say the pain is what produces the character to sustain life change and the ability to reach back through your pain to help others along the way.

So, when we become Eve, we must face our own dysfunction (sin). And this is the pivotal moment. Just like Eve, we know the promise. We know what was spoken over us. We know that God created us and that he wants us to live in freedom from shame. We were created for freedom. The problem is we get stuck in the middle over what God has said over our lives and the promise that is in the process of being fulfilled. We get stuck in the middle because the core of who we are craves Eve's perfection.

The birthplace of disappointment is false assumptions. These false assumptions drive thought patterns into false fantasies. I assumed that after college I would get a job that would make the student loan payments easier. I assumed that after marriage I would have children of my own. I assume that my children will outlive me. These assumptions leave a hole in my heart and can leave me disappointed with God when my plans are altered in any way. The birthplace of disappointment does not begin with God; it begins with the false assumptions we put on our own lives. The danger of assumption is striving for perfection that is not attainable within our own strength.

So how can we identify these snares of assumption that leave us reaching for a wisdom that was not intended? Can we gain discernment in this area?

The first step in gaining discernment is found in an action. In Genesis 3:6 it is written, "When the woman saw that the fruit of the tree was good for food and pleasing to the eye, and also desirable for gaining wisdom, she took some and ate it. She gave some to her husband, who was with her, and he ate it." We see Eve taking an action within her mind that begins to ignite and drive her senses. When our minds are driven by our senses, our minds take the place of God or the things God has spoken over us, as we see with Eve. The first step in identifying false assumptions within our lives is following our actions. Our actions will lead us to our true motives. It is a constant battle to keep our motives in line with what God has spoken over our lives. We begin to check our motives by asking ourselves:

- What am I indulging in?
- Am I deserving of anything good to happen in my life?
- Am I feeding into my guilt and shame with my actions in this season?
- Am I living in self-deprivation and hiding?

The next step in gaining discernment is to beware of secretive aspects of your life. Genesis 3:7 says, "Then the eyes of both of them were opened, and they realized they were naked; so they sewed fig leaves together and made coverings for themselves." Here we see Eve being driven by her senses, realizing her exposure, and hiding from the truth. When we feel exposed for who we really are, our initial response is to create a covering for ourselves. We reach for anything that will cover us: lies, manipulation, and gossip. Eve covered herself, and we create coverings in our lives as well. These coverings can take many forms. A common form of covering is to begin to hide aspects of our lives from the people we are closest to and to create an atmosphere of secrecy where there was openness before. Check your motives by asking yourself:

- What areas in my life have I stopped sharing with others?
- What areas of my life have I stopped praying for/communicating with God over?
- In what ways do I use my surroundings to hide from my current reality?

The snares of assumptions will also lead you into seclusion. Genesis 3:8–10 says, "Then the man and his wife heard the sound of the Lord God as he was walking in the garden in the cool of the day, and they hid from the Lord God among the trees of the garden. But the Lord God called to the man, 'Where are you?' He answered, 'I heard you in the garden, and I was afraid because I was naked; so I hid.'" Eve hides from God physically, but we know she is actually hiding from God emotionally and spiritually as well. Hiding and secrecy will always lead to loneliness and seclusion. Seclusion will always leave us susceptible to Satan. Seclusion will trick our minds into thinking we are stuck in our situation. And when we get stuck, we get stupid, acting on impulse alone.

- Am I acting out of character in this season?
- What is the root of my loneliness?
- Am I stuck in my current situation?

We then find ourselves in the snare of undermining the people we love. In Genesis 3:11–13 it is written, "And he said, 'Who told you that you were naked? Have you eaten from the tree that I commanded you not to eat from?' The man said, 'The woman you put here with me—she gave me some fruit from the tree, and I ate it.' Then the Lord God said to the woman, 'What is this you have done?' The woman said, 'The serpent deceived me, and I ate.'"

Here we see Adam blame Eve and Eve blame the Serpent. Both Adam and Eve are, in turn, blaming God for their actions. Adam blames God directly by calling out God's creation of woman. By Eve blaming the snake, she is indirectly placing the blame on God, the Creator of all things. Today we act the same way. Instead of looking in the mirror and owning up to our mistakes, we shift the blame to anyone and everyone around us. We internally blame God most often, creating resentment in our relationships as well as resentment toward God. When we go down the road of believing false assumptions within our lives, we end up unintentionally hurting the people we love.

- What are the resentments I currently hold within my relationships?
- What resentment do I secretly hold in my heart?
- What do I do with the blame I put on myself?

Assumption inevitably forces the need to mediate the situation. In Genesis 3:16 it is written, "To the woman he said, 'I will make your pains in childbearing very severe; with painful labor you will give birth to children. Your desire will be for your husband, and he will rule over you.'"

To mediate means to settle a dispute or to bring a truce between two parties. In the garden, Adam and Eve proved humans were unable to live a sinless life. They needed a mediator to bridge the gap between the law and God. Someone was needed to bring truce back to earth between God and man. God sent his son Jesus to earth to live a sinless life, die a sinner's death on a cross, and act as the mediator between God and man. Jesus defeated death and sin so man would never be separated from God again. Jesus is the redeemer of all people, accomplishing what Adam failed to do. Because of Jesus's blood and this mediation, humankind will never be separated from God and has no need to cover their sin.

- Do I need a mediator in my life?
- What situations have needed mediation throughout my life?
- Would Jesus truly die to redeem me of my sin?

The final snare of assumption leaves us to evaluate our situations. Genesis 4:1 says, "Adam made love to his wife Eve, and she became pregnant and gave birth to Cain. She said, 'With the help of the Lord I have brought forth a man.'"

Imperfection and falling short will come and go throughout our lives, leaving us in a constant state of evolution and change. I dare say one of the only aspects we have control of is the ability to look back at our situations and learn from them. It is in the

FACING OUR DYSFUNCTION

reflection of the rearview mirror that we can see our past situations from a different perspective. It is in these moments that we begin to understand our pain and God's perspective.

God never defined Eve by her sin. Her sin led her on a different path than she thought her life would take—a path marked by God's unconditional love and mercy instead of a path marked by perfection. Eve found herself experiencing extreme pain through the glory of extending the next generation. Love is not the absence of pain; it is the perception we acquire by pushing past the pain to experience our greatest potential. Eve teaches us through the pain and perseverance that we will passionately prevail and give the best of who we are to the next generation. Pain is progress. Pain is potential. Pain is penetrating through self to discover a love designed by the Creator before time began.

There is danger in striving for perfection that is not attainable. Jesus moves away from perfection toward our brokenness. Jesus does not take us out of our current situations—he meets us in them.

- When did you last take time to evaluate your current situations?
- How has God been challenging you through your pain?
- How has your pain propelled you to a different perspective?

It is okay not to be okay. We will have dysfunctional thoughts and actions, but it is how we respond to God that leads to freedom. Could it be every time we speak about Jesus, God is speaking directly to us? What if we serve a God who is that detailed, that loving, that intentional?

Until Jesus is enough in your life, no person or thing will ever be.

CHAPTER 6

The Hope of Redemption

Then the Lord God said to the woman, "What is this you have done?"
Genesis 3:13

Despite the doubt, shame, hiding, and guilt, we have a choice. We can live in it, or we can overcome it. For Eve, the beginning of overcoming her shame was a question from God: "What is this you have done?" This very question has pierced the souls of human beings since the garden. This creates a pull within our inner being. This questioning from God tears at our hearts and boggles our minds, creating a complex: Does God really exist? Does he speak to me? How could a story more than two thousand years old curse me today?

We have an intimate, loving God who is relentless in His pursuit of us and refuses to leave us alone. He is a God who continues to pursue us when we do not want to pursue him. This truth has rung throughout my lifetime and has been a foundational focal point of every human heart I have come across.

Eve was the only woman on earth to experience perfection. In a moment of uncertainty, she lost the vision God had for her life, but she never lost touch with God. Perfect love covers shame. That's what makes Christianity so beautiful, and that is what frees us from the bondage of shame and the obscurity of our hiding.

We will never be perfect, we will sin, and we all fall short, according to Romans 3:23. Instead of it leading to shame, we have a God who makes a covenant with us that is full of grace and love. His perfect love casts out fear (1 John 4:18). He covered us on the cross so we don't have to cover ourselves. He buried himself so we don't have to bury ourselves in guilt and shame and flaws. Unlike us, he conquered sin and rose from the grave, covering our transgressions and making us righteous. We get to live in the hope that does not put us to shame (Romans 5:5). We get to live in the hope that freely died for us so that we may be reconciled back to him from the moment we eat of the fruit.

Overcoming shame in our lives is not about working to make ourselves perfect, for we will never attain that perfection on our own. Overcoming shame is about understanding the gospel, the saving grace and mercy of Jesus Christ. It is understanding we are more sinful and flawed than we would ever fathom, but at the same time, we are more loved and accepted in Jesus Christ than we can ever comprehend. That is the profoundness of his provision: despite our sinful, flawed selves, he died for us. He died for the daughter who gave in to every vice, took every shortcut, and begged for the pain to come to an end. Eve's having and losing everything is a direct reflection of Jesus's sacrifice. He had everything and forfeited everything in a single moment to reverse the curse Eve brought on humanity. The truth is we do not know what it is like to live in perfection, but we know what it is like to wait and anticipate living in perfection.

So why is Eve revolutionary? Despite Eve's sin, her love relationship with her Creator grew stronger. God loved his creation in such a way he still used Eve to produce for the earth. Through the pain of childbirth, Eve became the mother of all nations and her genealogy is our genealogy. Through the pain and perseverance, Eve's passion for her Creator only grew. God is loving. God had to create pain for Eve, not out of punishment but out of remembrance of all he had done in her life. Every time a child is born, it is a reminder of the greatness of the Creator. Through Eve, we remember we deserved to be banished from the garden and

THE HOPE OF REDEMPTION

destroyed, not to be drawn close and to be died for. All of Eve's children are a foreshadow of the prophecy of the Child (Christ) to come die for our sins. I dare claim all our children are the fulfillment of that prophecy—the prophecy that Christ has risen from the grave and defeated death, and because of this we live with the Holy Spirit within.

Love is allowing the struggle and waiting on the other side, just as Christ waits for us in the heavenly realms. Jesus is working despite the twists and turns we take along the way. Jesus is the author and finisher of our faith, and our faith will not be made whole until we reach heaven. The bottom line is God loves our brokenness; he built his redemptive power upon it. Don't fight it. Do not try to make sense of it. Just love yourself through it. Allow yourself the same grace and love Jesus died for thousands of years ago.

> Therefore, since we have been justified through faith, we have peace with God through whom we have gained access by faith into this grace in which we now stand. And we boast in the hope of the glory of God. Not only so, but we also glory in our sufferings, because we know that suffering produces perseverance, perseverance character, and character hope. And hope does not put us to shame, because God's love has been poured out into our hearts through the Holy Spirit, who has been given to us. (Romans 5:1–5)

CHAPTER 7

Becoming Revolutionary

"We all, like sheep, have gone astray, each of us has turned to our own way; and the Lord has laid on him the iniquity of us all."
Isaiah 53:6

Eve's story is often defined by one moment. She sinned, and humanity was cursed. She would endure pain the rest of her life. But Eve is revolutionary because she overcame blame, shame, and hiding to live a life that was unappreciated in her time.

Remember, becoming revolutionary is being unappreciated in your time while leaving a legacy for the next generation. Eve is the first revolutionary woman because she acknowledged the process through the pain she experienced. God never defined Eve for her mistakes yet entrusted her to be the mother of the future generation. Our lives are not about our past mistakes. God meets us where we are, and His love gets us through, without dismissing the pain. We know that without the pain there is no purpose. The pain is the power that creates change in our lives. Instead of cursing God's name through the process, Eve learned to praise him through the pain.

We see Eve become revolutionary when she bore children for the first time. She experienced her punishment in full. All the while she praised God through her pain. The pain produced a product that declared victory over that which caused her to stumble. The output was beyond her wildest expectations. Eve is revolutionary because she shows us what perseverance truly is. It is being in perfection, falling short, and finding out that, when you are at the bottom, God is beneath your situation fighting for you. It is here we discover for ourselves that God is more real than ever. His love goes deeper than our problems. And his intimacy penetrates our very beings. It is in these moments he begins to transform our being back into the original creation that he intended all along—a worshiper in perfect communion with him.

We can become revolutionary when, in our shame and hiding, we realize that we do not have to fight our own way out but can be seen for who we truly are in front of the Lord. When we are being stripped away emotionally because the barriers are broken, remember that Christ took our shame, and he is not ashamed of us when we live in communion with him. He tells us that we become pure. And when we approach him in vulnerability, we become revolutionary. We become revolutionary when, instead of hiding and burying our feelings, we take our sins directly to Christ who bore them. We then come to a place where we can face our mistakes.

Eve could have lived her life in shame and hiding forever, and we probably would not have blamed her. We all face situations in which our initial response is shame. Adam and Eve's initial response to their shame was hiding. Hiding led to fear and fear led to obscurity. Hiding is the default to our sin. By hiding we deceive ourselves into a false sense of comfort and security that keeps us in bondage. These chains hold us back from seeing truth. These are the same chains that we wrap around ourselves by thinking we are not good enough, even though God created us to be enough.

We become revolutionary when we identify doubt and temptation and then combat doubt with trust—trusting that God will carry and propel us to our future. We are to trust God in the good, the bad, and the indifferent times, knowing that God is steadfast, and we are prone to drifting. Revolution lies within our ability to continue our faith in the unseen promises God has spoken over our lives amid our daily doubt and temptations.

Eve's character feels like a throw away. She is cast out of paradise by her own doing. She has the best of everything and ends up losing it all. We can point to God but subconsciously we know God was never at fault. Eve's story is for the person who feels cast away, the one in chains, in bondage, and engrossed in self-elevation. God will meet you in your weakness so you can live a life of worth and purpose found only in Him. This is what God does to show redemption for the first Adam (in Genesis) through the second Adam (Jesus).

Eve's revolution transcends time to create the next generation of believers. This genealogy eventually led to the birth of Jesus Christ. The one who conquered death and put the Serpent under his foot. He created man in perfection, he redeemed us when we broke it, and he restores us to the intended glory for eternity when we call upon his name. Christ took our punishment, yet he still uses us because he redeemed us and continues to show his love and power for generations to come.

Being revolutionary is not about a status. It is about slipping out of mediocrity and living with purpose and passion every day. It is the most selfless aspect of who you are . . . dying for a cause you will never see. It is feeling the weight of the sacrifice of the generations that have gone before you and being compelled to live with a renewed purpose throughout your time on earth. Being revolutionary means you can look back over your life and know the cause was worth the struggle. It is dying with the satisfaction that you gave it your all. Being revolutionary is having hope in things that are unseen and uncertain. It is a mindset that, to live or die, it is all gain. It is being proud of the roots, the pain, and the struggle. To be revolutionary is to be proud to be a descendant of Eve, a perseverer whose life illustrates both perfection and redemption. Believe wholeheartedly that Jesus can also take your redemption and turn you into perfection. He calls you to be an overcomer—not defeated, but a conqueror. You are a victor because, in him, you have won.

In him, I am who he says I am. Defy the lies of the Enemy. "God says . . ."

I am a child of God.
"To all who believed him and accepted him, he gave the right to become children of God." (John 1:12 NLT)

I am a joint heir with Christ.
"Since we are His children, we are His heirs. In fact, together with Christ we are heirs of God's glory." (Romans 8:17 NLT)

I am a temple, a dwelling place of God.
"Don't you realize that your body is the temple of the Holy Spirit who lives in you and was given to you by God?" (1 Corinthians 6:19 NLT)

I am a new creation.
"Anyone who belongs to Christ has become a new person. The old life is gone; a new life has begun!" (2 Corinthians 5:17 NLT)

I am a threat to the devil.
"I have given you authority to trample on snakes and scorpions and to overcome all the power of the enemy; nothing will harm you." (Luke 10:19)

I am free from condemnation.
"There is no condemnation for those who belong to Christ Jesus." (Romans 8:1 NLT)

I may approach God with confidence.
"Because of Christ and our faith in him, we can now come boldly and confidently into God's presence." (Ephesians 3:12 NLT)

I am complete in Christ.
"You also are complete through your union with Christ, who is the head over every ruler and authority." (Colossians 2:10 NLT)

I have been redeemed and forgiven from all my sins.
"He has rescued us from the kingdom of darkness and transferred us into the kingdom of His dear Son, who purchased our freedom and forgave our sins." (Colossians 1:13–14 NLT)

I am the light and no longer belong to the darkness.
"You are all children of the light and children of the day. We do not belong to the night or to darkness." (1 Thessalonians 5:5)

I am chosen and treasured.
"For you are the people who hold to the Lord your God. The Lord your God has chosen you out of all the people on the earth to be His people, His treasured possession." (Deuteronomy 7:6)

I am beautiful and flawless.
"You are altogether beautiful, my darling; there is no flaw in you." (Song of Songs 4:7)

I am strong and have peace.
"The Lord gives strength to His people; the Lord blesses His people with peace." (Psalm 29:11)

I am accepted.
"Accept one another then, just as Christ accepted you, in order to bring praise to God." (Romans 15:7)

I am more than a conqueror.
"In all these things we are more than conquerors through him who loved us." (Romans 8:37)

I am confident and fearless.
"For God has not given us a spirit of fear and timidity, but of power, love, and self-discipline." (2 Timothy 1:7 NLT)

I am worthy of His love.
"They will walk with me, dressed in white, for they are worthy." (Revelation 3:4)

I am loved unconditionally.
"Neither height nor depth, nor anything else in all creation, will be able to separate us from the love of God that is in Christ Jesus our Lord." (Romans 8:39)

I am created in the image of God.
"God created human beings in His own image." (Genesis 1:27 NLT)

I am a citizen of heaven.
"But we are citizens of heaven, where the Lord Jesus Christ lives. And we are eagerly waiting for him to return as our Savior." (Philippians 3:20 NLT)

I am free.
"The power of the Holy Spirit has made me free from the power of sin and death. This power is mine because I belong to Christ Jesus." (Romans 8:2 NLV)

I am his masterpiece.
"Then the Lord God made man from the dust of the ground. And He breathed into his nose the breath of life. Man became a living being." (Genesis 2:7 NLV)

I am who he says I am because he is the eternal I Am.

BECOMING REVOLUTIONARY

Dear Reader,

You have just read the story of Eve as perceived by one viewpoint. Is this the whole truth about the story of Adam and Eve? Jesus said to seek and you will find the answers you need for life. Truth is found when you look for yourself.

This section is designed to help you discover the story of Eve as recorded in the Bible. It consists of seven chapters that you can study on your own or with a small discussion group.

You may be surprised to learn that this ancient story will be applicable to your life today. No matter where we live or what century we find ourselves living in, God's Word is truth. It is as relevant today as it was yesterday. In it we find our lineage and our hope.

Chapter 1: Becoming Eve
Scripture Focus: Genesis 2:4–4:2
Reflection Questions:
If Eve were sitting next to you today, what questions would you have for her?

_____
_____
_____
_____

Do mistakes from your past define who you are today? If so, how? If not, how have you kept them from doing so?

_____
_____
_____
_____
_____

In what ways are you like Eve?

Chapter 2: Doubt
Scripture Focus: Genesis 3:1–3
Reflection Questions:
In what ways do you feel God really loves you?

Describe what trying to succeed without God would look like. What problems might be encountered?

In what ways do you feel you're in control of your own destiny?

Are you in control of your own destiny?

Identify the false fantasies within your life.

Chapter 3: False Fantasy and Sin
Scripture Focus: Genesis 3:4–6
Reflection Questions:
What do you daydream about?

How do your desires shape your actions?

Is what you are dreaming about a true promise of God, or is it something that only brings self-glorification or gratification?

Is true change and character development a battle worth fighting in your life? Why or why not?

Is God worth your whole desire? Why or why not?

Chapter 4: The Consequence—Shame and Hiding
Scripture Focus: Genesis 3:7–13
Reflection Questions:
What does hiding look like in your life?

BECOMING REVOLUTIONARY

How do you allow God to begin to change your natural patterns?
_____
_____
_____
_____

How did you end up where you currently are?
_____
_____
_____
_____

How do you pick up the pieces of your life and continue with what you have?
_____
_____
_____
_____

How do you take control of your life when you feel so helpless?
_____
_____
_____
_____

How do you continue living and leading a fulfilling life after you have hurt so many?
_____
_____
_____
_____

Chapter 5: Facing Our Dysfunction
Scripture Focus: Genesis 4:1
Reflection Questions:
When did you last take time to evaluate your current situations?

What are you indulging in?

Are you deserving of anything good to happen in your life?

Are you feeding into your guilt and shame with your actions in this season? If so, how?

Are you living in self-deprivation and hiding? If so, in what ways?

BECOMING REVOLUTIONARY

How has God been challenging you through your pain?

How has your pain propelled you to a different perspective?

What are the resentments you currently hold within your relationships?

What resentment do you secretly hold in your heart?

What do you do with the blame you put on yourself?

Chapter 6: The Hope of Redemption
Scripture Focus: Romans 5:1–5
Reflection Questions:
What does love look like in your life?

_____
_____
_____
_____
_____

How has Jesus redeemed your emotions, thought patterns, and lifestyle?

_____
_____
_____
_____
_____

Chapter 7: Becoming Revolutionary
Scripture Focus: Isaiah 53:6
Reflection Questions:
What attributes of Eve make her revolutionary?

_____
_____
_____

What attributes do you possess that make you revolutionary?

_____
_____
_____
_____

Read the I AM statements aloud daily to shatter the lies with the truth.

Shatter the lies with truth and dig deeper into more resources from Ellis Ministries by going to www.ellisministries.org.

ORDER INFORMATION

To order additional copies of this book, please visit
www.redemption-press.com.
Also available on Amazon.com and BarnesandNoble.com
Or by calling toll free 1-844-2REDEEM.

CPSIA information can be obtained
at www.ICGtesting.com
Printed in the USA
LVHW051117030322
712397LV00011B/1083